Behind the Motometer

Robert I. Frey

plus
one bonus tale by
Trudy Frey

Behind the Motometer

Published through Lulu Press, Inc.

ISBN: 978-1-105-56619-6

Forward
Bruce Eric Frey

One of my earliest memories is of my father's 1917 Model T Ford. I remember being almost three years old and gazing upward, looking beyond the gracefully curving fenders, past the eye-like headlights to the top of the flat grill. Perched on a narrow pedestal at the front of the hood, gleaming like Grandpa's silver pocket watch, the motometer beckoned. *

To modern drivers the motometer might seem to be a mere ornament, a decoration, a stylish radiator cap. But until the technological advances of the 1920's, (interior gauges and pressurized engine cooling,) the Boyce motometer served a crucial function. It measured the temperature of the radiator's water vapor. Driving the Model T on hot summer days, my father would have one eye on the road, and one eye on the motometer. Sometimes he'd have to stop the old car and race to steal water from some stranger's garden hose or birdbath before the radiator boiled over.

I also have early memories of my father telling stories. At antique car rallies, Grange meetings, and after church I would find him centered in a cluster of laughing people. With each new audience I'd hear the same tales repeated. They evolved with time, losing a minor detail here, gaining an embellishment there. The story, though the same, grew better. The best tales gained a reputation of their own; at picnics and farm sales there were requests for the favorites: "Hey, Bob, tell the one 'bout your blimp-chasin' dog," or "Hey, Bob, tell the one 'bout the time the rat climbed up inside old Cyrus's overalls."

He has published many of these stories on the back page of the Lehigh Valley Region of the Antique Automobile Club of America's newsletter, under the column titled, "Behind the Motometer." In celebration of my parents' fiftieth wedding anniversary, we have compiled a selection of them. Enjoy the read.

---

* It spoke to me and said: "Paint the cars! A Model T should be black, not blue! There's a wide brush full of black enamel soaking in a can of paint thinner *right here in the garage*. And when you're done painting the Model T, and the Model A, you can paint Daddy's brand new, emerald–green, 1967 Chevy Impala! Grab the brush with both hands. That's right. Now, spash that paint around. Excellent! Daddy is sure gonna be surprised – and maybe someday he'll tell a story about it!"

There was an old farmer from here,
Who farmed with a two cylinder Deere.
An old car and a truck,
A good wife, boys and luck,
And paid off the farm free and clear.

Bob Frey

Acknowledgement

Thank you, Albina Morris and Mary Jane Pokojni, for putting *Behind the Motometer* in our antique car club's newsletter, "Body Squeaks."

And special thanks to friends, Trish Becker, Sue Tintle and Norbert McGuire, for proofreading these stories.

Behind the Motometer

Stories of old cars,
singular people
and multiple dogs

Robert I. Frey

plus
one bonus tale by
Trudy Frey

Valentine Cake

Mrs. Decker was just the nicest lady. She always asked about the family and about the things that most interested us. Once she asked how my wife and I met, for she knew Trudy was from Philadelphia and college educated and I was from the boondocks and had barely made it through high school.

We asked her why she had asked us this. She replied, "Oh, some people collect salt shakers and some people collect antique cars, but I collect information. It doesn't take up any space in the garage and does make for very interesting conversation."

The local Grange had a cake baking contest. (The Grange is a nationwide fraternal lodge with local units involved in civic issues in rural areas.) They called upon the County Home Economist to be an impartial judge and my mother's cake won first place. The Judge announced that cake number three, the walnut cake with white icing had won. My mother stepped up, accepted the blue ribbon and told the judge that cake number three was indeed her cake, but she had baked a *banana* cake, not a *walnut* cake. The judge consulted her score cards and said, "No, cake number three is most definitely a walnut cake with a score of ninety-eight." My mother was a great cake baker but never, ever, made walnut cakes. She, as a girl, had to pick up "shell bark" walnuts and pound on them and did not care for walnuts at all. I thought to myself that the judge, who was only a couple of years out of college, certainly had a lot of nerve to argue with my mother over a cake she had baked.

I recalled this when I met that girl again at a YWCA dance a couple of months later. I discovered that she was pretty nice after all, had a good job and a brand new 1956 Plymouth Belvedere. We dated for five years, eventually married and now years later when she bakes a cake, she usually makes a banana cake, and we laugh about what kind of cake it is.

This is our Valentine story, but with a P.S.

Since the first printing of this collection, we have learned that there was, in fact, a walnut cake in the contest. It was baked by Esther Fair Heritage. See page 8 for the recipe.

Cursors and Cursers

I write this with a ball-point pen (invented circa 1945) on a yellow tablet (papyrus paper invented circa 3000 BC). An IBM computer with word processor sets idly in the living room. I recently took a two day computer course and will continue, pen in hand, with my old way. *

My maternal grandfather, Isaac Hance, operated on this same principle. He drove horses until 1926 when, at Grandma's insistence, they finally bought a new Star car. Thus, he was pushed, kicking and screaming, into the 20th century. BUT, he kept his beloved driving team. The Star, incidentally, had cut glass flower vases, a Waltham clock and nickel plated bumper. It was quite nice. Grandpa was a horse and trace chain man in a nuts and bolts age. I am a pen and paper man in a bits and bytes age. The clutch pedal meant as much to Grandpa as a control "C" key does to me.

One evening Ike and his Sarah came back from visiting Aunt Suzie. He left Grandma off at the house and put the car in the tool shed, now the garage. But he forgot the control "C" (i.e. clutch) and ran right into the work bench and kerosene barrel screaming, "Whoa, dammit whoa!" He examined the damage -- a bent fender and dents in the hood. An ax and a mall had fallen out of the rafters, (A mall, you twenty-first century people, is a heavy wooden hammer -- not a place to spend money.) Grandpa shut the garage doors, went to the barn and started to curry comb his horses -- and that's the honest truth, or so they told me.

Arthur Frey with his horse, Dewey, and his grandson, Bob.

* Special thanks to Denise Conroy for typing and archiving these essays and to Bob's grandson, Caleb Frey, for "digitalizing" the old photographs for publication.

7

Lloyd

Lloyd was a precocious kid and so the family would send him off to visit their farming relations every summer. He couldn't wait until school was out for he loved the outdoors. After high school he got a city job with a large Ford agency. Eventually, the dealer sent him and four other guys with cash money (Henry Ford wanted cash) to bring back a batch of new Model T's from the New Jersey assembly plant.

He got to know the guys at the shipping dock. Then, as now, Ford made police specials and Lloyd persuaded them to save him a Ford T that the Bayonne Police Department had rejected due to an ill-fitting top.

Now, on weekends, Lloyd could visit his country cousins and get to see the local country girls. He became a bit of a hero, also, after rescuing a team of runaway horses and later single-handedly pushing a tractor out of a burning hay barn.

Before long he got to going "steady" with a fair farmer's daughter who lived way out in Warren County some 65 miles from his "Joisey City." He could make the trip in an hour and a half although "Jugtown Mountain" slowed him down a bit. He made up for it going down hill, however, with both gas and spark levers all the way back. Magneto headlights do get brighter the faster you go.

One Saturday afternoon, young Esther persuaded Lloyd to teach her to drive, and she happened to get a little too close to the edge and over they went into an open ditch with the Model T on its side.

This was back when ditches were still being dug by hand, and the workmen scrambled out of there for their very lives. Nobody was hurt. They picked up the Model T and the fenders all sprung right back in place (thanks to Henry Ford's vanadium alloys) and it did not spoil the car or the romance one little bit.

Author's Note... Living proof exists (although Lloyd and Esther have now passed on to their rewards) in two children, nine grandchildren and lots of nice great grandkids with more on the way.

Esther's Walnut Cake Recipe

½ cup butter	2/3 cup milk
1 cup sugar	½ cup butter
2 eggs	1 2/3 cup flour
1 egg yolk	1 ½ teaspoons baking powder
1 tsp vanilla	2/3 cup finely chopped walnuts

Beat until light: sugar, butter, eggs. Then add walnuts. Add milk alternately, with flour and baking soda. Beat around two minutes with mixer. Pour into 2-8" cake pan. Bake 350 degrees F for 30 min or until done. Ice with your favorite frosting.

Bird of Wonder

"When the Bird of Wonder dies – the Maiden Phoenix,
her ashes new, create another heir as great in admiration as herself."
-- Tennison

The Raub sawmill operation was much like the fabled Phoenix Bird. It always arose from the ashes of destruction or more aptly *with* the ashes of destruction, and every generation a family member took over the operation. During the Civil War the mill made packing crates for cannon balls. They invested their profits in an iron mine and the Depression of 1873 just about wiped them out. They planted peach orchards and made peach baskets until the blight wiped out the trees. By the time of Teddy Roosevelt's "great little war" they were able to successfully bid on packing crates once more. Grandpa Albert then built a big American mansion. He was a visionary – a true opportunist, but fell on hard times until World War I came along (the war to end all wars) and he made a lot of money and invested in the stock market. He built a modern sawmill which burned a year or two after the stock market crashed. By 1939 the Raubs had gotten back up on their feet and "Link" had acquired a contract for his generation to build crates once more.

"Link's" son Ken grew up around the sawmill and every day after school he fed slab wood into the ancient steam engine which ran the mill. Father and son became very close and when Ken got to high school, his father encouraged him to play football even though they had to hire somebody to work in Ken's place every afternoon.

Ken became a star halfback and began going steady with a pretty cheerleader. He borrowed his father's brand new 1939 Buick Super to go to the spring prom. Ken and his girl did a bit of "necking" out in front of her home after the dance. Finally they realized how late it was and Ken hurried home. He took a gradual curve entirely too fast and rolled that new car into the ditch in front of our house. He crawled out completely unhurt and walked home to break the news to his parents. (This was in the days long before a local police force existed and before every accident was a bonanza for some tow truck operator).

The next morning Link and Ken came back with their 1928 International truck and my father pulled the Buick out of the ditch with his John Deere tractor. They dragged the Buick up planks onto the log truck and fastened it down with chain binders. My father said, "It's certainly too bad about your new car, Link." Link's reply was, "Oh, we can always get another car, but we can't get another Ken," and he hugged his son. Then my father put his arm around eight-year-old me and gave me a hug too. I looked up and I thought I saw tears in the eyes of both grown men as they hugged their sons. At the time I did not understand those tears, but today I do.

Hardscrabble Mountain Farm

It was a big family, and they did their best on the hardscrabble mountain farm. They always managed to have meat on the table. The bigger kids looked after the others and helped mother with the garden and chores. Mother ruled the roost when father was off cutting mine timbers.

This particular night, mother had gone off with a neighbor lady and father hadn't gotten home yet. Chores and dishes were all finished when a shiny new Packard Phaeton came up the lane. The boys all ran out to see it go by, but it *stopped!* Out stepped a nicely dressed young man who asked if their sister was at home. The boys did have to admit their sister was pretty, but that Packard was a whole lot nicer. They examined themselves in the shiny hubcaps with the red spots. They stood on the running board and looked in at the real leather seats. They even crawled under it to examine the thing.

Sis was elated when she realized the driver was an acquaintance who came to court her. However, she did not dare to leave the baby of the family who was asleep in the crib. Going for a ride was out of the question.

So they all settled down on the porch with Sis and her suitor on the swing and six brothers whittling or playing marbles just off the 'stoop'. Eventually the man tosses the Packard keys to Jack, the oldest boy, and suggests he take all the kids for a nice ride.

Ecstatic, they piled into the car and off they went. Jack drove around the bend, slammed on the brakes and Buff crawled up on the left front fender with the double-barrel 12 gauge he's sneaked aboard. After all, Pappy always said, "Take the gun along boys, if you want meat on the table." So off they went again with Buff sprawled on the fender, gun over the headlight brace, and his feet back on the running board. This was the approved method of hunting for night rabbits with their old Dodge truck.

Down toward the lake they went and pretty soon the headlights picked up a goose in the road. "KA-BOOM" went Buff's gun, he jumped off and gave the goose's neck a good jerk and got back in the Packard with it.

About halfway around the lake the goose woke up and started flapping and flopping at everybody. It made several laps around the inside of the car shedding feathers everywhere. At about this point the gun went off (two barrels, remember?) right up through the canvas roof. Jack stopped the car and everybody, goose included, piled out. Nobody was hurt, just mighty scared! After the gun smoke cleared, they got back in the car and went straight home. They parked the Packard and all silently went to bed. To this day, Sis doesn't know why that nice young man never came back... but we do!

Dogs

There is a book entitled "Why Dogs Chase Cars" and basically it says it's because they lack trigger fingers and opposable thumbs to tie hangman's nooses or to turn on gas jets. Personally, I think they do it just for the thrill of it.

When I was a kid my Grandpa Frey had a German Shepherd that chased cars. He caught one once or at least he caught the tire. He bit through a bald 4.25 x 19 (we are again back to 19 inch wheels in 2012) and hung on. It flipped him over and the car ran right over his nose. Everyone thought this was pretty funny, except the motorist with a flat tire. Grandpa said old "Shep" gave up chasing cars then and there.

I've had quite a few good dogs in my lifetime. As a kid it was "Chippy" who would tear the house apart if he heard a mouse. Later there was "Bozo" who loved to ride on the operator's platform of our 1938 John Deere. We had "Nemo" who chased Goodyear Blimps until they disappeared over the horizon.

At one time we had "Betsy" a nice Brittany spaniel who patiently waited for our kid's school bus, but whose septic ears stunk so badly we could hardly stand it. Then there was "Dingo" that spent a lot of time licking his butt on the yellow line in the middle of the country road. He ended up just like "Patches" who had a habit of crossing interstate 78. "Red Dog" was a really nice pet who just loved to ride in my 49 Chevy truck. His only vice was to go to the town of Alpha to visit the lady dogs. Then I would drive through the back alleys calling his name and blowing the horn. He would appear and after a good scolding show a lot more contrition than Elliot Spitzer. We had "Burkey" who could spot a groundhog a half mile away. "Lucky", "Perky" and "Penny" came later. Somewhere along the line a retiring farmer gave me a Border collie. "Laddy" was supposed to round up cows, but all he really liked to do was chase cats. He would not bother with rats, mice or groundhogs.

About 15 years ago I decided I really needed a good cow dog and got "John" a registered Australian Red Heeler from a breeder. Somebody in Australia got the bright idea to breed the narrow minded, and wimpy Border Collies to Dingos. These Australian wild dogs spend their time chasing kangaroos and avoid getting kicked in the head. The result was a red, medium sized dog that bred true.

"John" had a great sense of humor, knew over 30 words, loved to ride on my all-terrain vehicle, catch Frisbees, work with cattle and he kept me company. We buried "John" on Palm Sunday behind the barn in a bed of straw with his toys and a Frisbee. And, he never, ever, chased cars, lady dogs, blimps or cats.

It's Time to Milk the Cows

Furman came in from the field because it was time to milk the cows. He went straight to the house for some milk and cookies and Louise told him he would have to go to town to get her some vanilla extract. "I can't go now, it's milking time! Can't you use something else?" "No, I've got to bake this cake for the church social tonight," she responded. "Yeah, but it's milking time," he said. "Ok, I'll get the kids to chase the cows in the barn and I'll put the milkers together for you if you'll just go to Central Supermarket and get me the vanilla." So Furman grabbed a handful of cookies and jumped into this red 1948 Ford Pickup (Sanford and Son had one just like it) and headed for town, all the while grumbling that it was time to milk the cows.

He found the bottle of vanilla, paid the clerk and started to get into his farm truck, when he realized there was a strange guy sitting in it. "What are you doing in my truck?" asked Furman. "Because, *you're* taking me to New York," was the answer. "I can't take you to New York, it's time to milk the cows!" "Oh yes you will," said the stranger as he waved his pistol. "I don't know how to get to New York. I've never been to New York!" "Get in and drive - *or else...*" said the stranger with the gun.

So they headed east on the Brunswick Pike passed old Greenwich Church, up Kennedy Hill with Furman grumbling that it was milking time. As they approached Slow Joe's Gas Station and Tourist Cabins, Furman realized there were two New Jersey State Police cars parked there side by side with the officers talking. He pulled his ten year old pickup in right beside the black and white police cruisers, mustered up all his courage and told the gun man, "There is your ride to New York. Now you get out of my truck. It's time to milk the cows!"

I've Got a Question

They call me Bruce Boy and I lived with a couple of big folks known as Bob Daddy and Trudy Mommy. They can't understand much of what I say... Boy, are they dumb! I can understand everything they say, but I don't let on that I can. It makes things more interesting.

Trudy Mommy goes a lot and takes me in the car with her. It's my job to see that she stays on the right side of the yellow lines in the road.

Once she left me in her '56 Plymouth with push-button transmission and told me not to touch the shiny brake lever while she got out to take a photo. But I'd seen her touch it, and figured it wouldn't hurt if I just gave it a tiny tap with my finger. She certainly did run to catch up to the car as it coasted away! I still don't know why she got so angry because I did a real good job of steering.

Bob Daddy has what he calls a Model T. He takes it for rides and honks the oogah horn at all the pretty ladies. They smile and wave and he likes that. Once in a while it boils just like Grandma's teapot, and Bob Daddy gets very upset.

Bob Daddy told Trudy Mommy that as long as she was going to have another baby, he thought he should be able to get a Model A Coupe. All it needed was some fixing and a paint job! I don't know why on earth he would want a Model A as long as he had a perfectly good Model T, or why she wanted another baby as long as she had me. They must both be nuts!

While they were waiting for delivery of that new baby, Bob Daddy towed his Model A home and put it in the garage. In the spring the men were painting the barn, and I got a paint brush and started painting the Model A. Bob Daddy got so mad he chased me, but I ran and hid under the bed. Tell me good folks; are ALL antique car people really nuts???

Hay There

There was once a popular song, "Hey there, you with the stars in your eyes," by Patty Paige, and Kent had stars in his eyes about his Saturday night date.

After the morning milking, barn chores and a big breakfast he got his fairly new red and white 1957 Pontiac Convertible out of the wagon shed. His sisters kidded him when he borrowed his mom's Electrolux and vacuumed the slate dust off of the canvas top and cleaned the interior. He washed the car and then used the milk house chlorinated detergent to scrub the whitewalls.

His father was sharpening the hay-mower knives and urging him to "hurry-up" and get to the field before the hay got too dry and all the leaves fell off. So Kent cranked up the Farmall Super C, and took 2 flat wagons "over the highway" to the rented hay field. He hooked up to the steel wheeled hay rake and set off going round and round trying to stay awake and finished just as his father arrived with the 1946 Chevy stake-body truck. Then they ate the lunch Mom had prepared and enjoyed the ice tea from the thermos jug. They hooked the wagon behind the New Holland baler, managed to get its Wisconsin engine started and set off with Dad driving the tractor and Kent stacking bales on the wagons. They then unloaded** the hay from the wagons onto the stake-body truck, (which had a half-dozen twelve-foot-long wooden planks sticking out the back in order to hold more bales); Kent stacked them as high as he dared, two bales higher than the cab of the truck, but there would be no need to worry about losing any bales, as the hay would be secured by several long, brown, hemp ropes.

By the time they had the truck loaded it was almost milking time and Kent's father needed to get back to the barn. He climbed onto the tractor and put it in fourth gear. As drove out of the field, he turned and yelled to Kent, "Just be sure and tie them bales down good and tight before you head-on home!"

Having worked hard all day, cleaning his car in the morning and stacking (and re-stacking) bales in the hot afternoon sun, Kent suddenly found himself tired. Dog-tired. He could barely keep his eyes open. While he was anxious to be on time for his date that night, he reasoned there was some benefit to being well rested for it. There was also no point in hurrying home just yet, as it meant more cows for him to milk. So he decided to lie down in the shade under the truck to rest a moment. (All farm dogs know there is a nice cool breeze under a truck or wagon.) He meant to take a brief nap – ten or fifteen minutes - but when he awoke, the sun was far lower in the sky than it should have been.

** Note I did not use the term "off-loaded," as it hadn't been invented yet.

Kent jumped into the truck and headed home. When he got to the intersection of Route 22 he had to wait for a break in the traffic. He finally saw an opening, floored it in low-low, and promptly lost a half dozen bales right in the middle of the highway. Kent knew he was in trouble. When a black Lincoln slid to a stop and three big guys in gangster zoot suits leaped out, Kent thought he was in *REALLY BIG TROUBLE,* but the men, shouting and swearing, grabbed the bales, threw them off to the shoulder of the road, jumped back in the Lincoln, and roared off.

"What should I do?" Kent wondered, sweat beading on his forehead. "What *can* I do?"   Try as he could, there was no way he could throw those sixty-pound bales back on top of the truck. And he couldn't just leave them there on the side of the four-lane highway! Just then, a neighbor lady came by. Kent stopped her and yelled, "Get my Dad! Get my Dad!" He knew his father would be angry; he might even punish him by making him do extra chores and Kent would probably miss his date. But at least Dad would know what to do. His father would come with the farm pick-up truck, throw the bales onto the bed, take them home, and the problem (other than the punishment,) would be over.

After what seemed like an eternity his father arrived, but he didn't come in the pick-up. Dad arrived in Kent's nice, clean, red and white, 1957 Pontiac convertible, its top folded down. Without a word, the old man threw the bales into the back seat, and with hayseeds flying, he gunned the engine and roared back to the barn. Kent stood at the side of the road, coughing from the dust and thinking, "I guess I'd better tie down the rest of the bales."

Kent was a little late for his big date with that girl he had met through 4-H, but she was nice about it and they hit it off quite well... hayseeds on the seats and all. She must have seen something good in this bumbling farm kid because they married a couple of years later, had three boys and a girl, all of whom helped make hay on the farm.

Trudy's Truck Story

The following story was written by my wife, Trudy, and published in July 1982 issue of Pennsylvania Farmer Magazine. – Bob Frey

Farm Truck with a Mind of Its Own

Almost every farm has a pickup truck. It is a useful, necessary vehicle. But ours is a 1946 Chevy and it makes me nervous. Or vice versa. We avoid each other.

The truck is my husband's and it runs, (most of the time,) back and forth from the house to the barn. It works best on mild, sunny days. In winter, starting is unpredictable, so it's best to wear warm clothes and never depend on the battery. The truck won't start in hot weather either, as it is prone to a mysterious engine malady my husband refers to as "vapor lock." Rainy days are an issue as the windshield wipers only work going downhill.

Other farm wives can jump in a pickup and go. I've tried that and sometimes it turns into an unforgettable trip. Like the time a little Volkswagen got hooked onto the back bumper. I couldn't see anything behind me, but there was this funny little "beep, beep, beep." While the nice young man stood on the bumper to get them apart, I inched forward. A yell! I stopped and found his leg was caught between the bumpers. Several people helped lift the Volkswagen and we went our separate ways.

Then on a one-hundred-degree August afternoon, when I was in my oldest and skimpiest outfit, busily canning tomatoes, the phone rang. My husband said, "Will you go to the butcher shop before it closes? Our beef is ready. Take the truck. It will hold all the meat from our cow." I didn't want to drive the truck. "I'll even start it for you," he pleaded. So off I went, with my two young sons, praying the truck would run. I carefully parked it on a hill when I got there, hoping it would make the starting easier.

After loading the bed of the truck with our farm-raised hamburger, chip steaks, and sirloins, we climbed into the cab, but the truck traveled no farther than a silent glide down the little hill. "No problem," said the butcher, "I'll get in my van and give you a push." He pushed and pushed. A block away there was a dip in the road. The pickup went down and the van went up and the bumpers were locked together. A large crowd gathered. I went back into the store and called home. We pulled and pried with everything, including heavy meat cleavers.

We got the trucks apart just as my father-in-law arrived. He carefully unfolded a canvas and covered the thawing beef. Confidently, he stepped into the pickup. "Forgot to tell you," he said, "We put in a new switch. What used to be on is off. Turn the key to what used to be off and it will be on."

Is it any wonder that I drive a car and leave the trucks for the farmers in the family? We have antique cars, too. But that's another story.

Trudy with baby Bruce and 1946 Chevy Farm Truck

(Note the leg [Bob's?] in front of garage door on right.)

Sons Robbie and Bruce with Red-Dog, pumpkins and 1949 Chevy

Changes

They say the only thing that does not change is change itself. I can think of a few exceptions, however. I still farm the land where my great-grandfather lived. No change there.

About a mile from Frey's Hill Farm is the small hamlet of Carpentersville. In the last one hundred years, two homes burned and one new house was built. Not much change there either.

And of course, human nature never changes.

In the late nineteenth century, this little town was self-contained: two quarries, two lime kilns, one sawmill, one distillery (Jersey Lightning), a grist mill, post office, school, chapel, railroad station and a country store. The coming of the automobile did most certainly change *this*, I must admit.

The little general store either had what you needed or could get it the next day by Railway Express. Warm bread came every morning on the 7:05 train from a bakery in Phillipsburg. Clams, oysters and crabs, (in season), arrived on ice. Our folks lived well then, as now. No change. The store held everything from pickles and candies to overalls and Brown's Beach vests. Of course, human nature being what it is – the women liked to shop elsewhere. No change, again.

Carpentersville – from a postcard dated 1907

Charlotte got Ike to take her to the train station so she could go shopping in Philadelphia at Wanamaker's store. She said she needed a gift for Pauline's wedding. "Don't you want to go along?" "No. I've got more important things to do," replied Ike. "OK, but be sure to meet me at the five-of-five train, and don't you dare forget!" He took her to the train in the buggy, came back home, unhooked the horse, put it in the barn, and took a good long nap. Nice and quiet around the house. Sound familiar?

Ike awoke, made himself some lunch and decided to oil the harness. He then washed and polished the buggy, including the spoke wheels. Next he curry-combed the horse and washed its mane and tail. Dark clouds rolled over the hills and a curtain of hard rain stormed toward the farm. Ike quickly led the clean horse back into the barn and pushed the shining buggy into the shed. He chamoised away the water droplets before they left marks. How many times have you washed your car and hated to get it dirty immediately?

Ike looked at his Ingersoll pocket watch and it was 4:30 and so he went into the house and grabbed two umbrellas and walked that mile to meet the afternoon train from Philadelphia. The train was right on schedule, the conductor lowered the iron steps and Great Grandma got off, all smiles and full of talk about her day and the great bargains she had acquired. (Sound familiar?) He handed her one umbrella and picked up her packages. They walked out of the train station with her chatting merrily away and only then did she ask where he put the horse and buggy.

They walked home together in a drizzle, and as the sun broke through, a rainbow appeared in the east with one end right over their farmhouse. And so, as in all good fables, Ike and Charlotte lived happily ever after. But can you imagine the conversation on the way back home? I bet you can. Faces change with each generation. People don't.

Ike and Charlotte Frey

Land of Opportunity

The land of opportunity was where he planned to go. Also Fritz figured he would end up being cannon fodder if he stayed in Germany which always had been involved in the periodic European wars. So he saved his money and with his family's help made the arrangements with an uncle in New York. He traveled in steerage, made it through the Ellis Island physical only to learn that the uncle had died.

What to do? He was in a strange country, couldn't speak the language, and as a teenager he was really just a kid. He was sleeping under a bridge when he awoke to hear a garbage man speaking to his horse in German. Fritz ran up to the man and explained his plight. After scratching his mustache the man said, " Alright kid, you help me today picking up garbage from the hotels and restaurants and I will see what I can do." Fritz worked as hard as he could and he had never worked harder. When the wagon was full the owner took him back across the Hudson to his farm in Secaucus, NJ. Fritz received a good supper, a place to sleep and the next day a pair of rubber boots and was put to work slopping the hogs. The garbage man and his young wife had a couple of small kids who helped with the farm chores and gradually Fritz picked up American English from them. With Fritz helping back on the farm, the garbage man was able to buy a bigger wagon, pick up more restaurants and put on more hogs.

All was going well and then the garbage man died. The widow asked Fritz to stay on as working manager and the arrangement worked pretty well for a couple of years. Then Fritz married her and eventually had a couple of kids by her. And then she died.

Gradually her older children were able to do more and more of the hard work. After a few years Fritz married the garbage man's oldest daughter and had some more kids. Meanwhile the sows were having piglets, 8 or 10 at a time, and Fritz bought chain drive Mack trucks to pick up even more garbage. When the government mandated that all garbage be cooked as a public health safeguard, Fritz's operation was big enough to afford the necessary boilers and to then "buy out" smaller pig farms and thus expand even more. It was said that if you married into Fritz's family they gave you, as a wedding gift, a pair of rubber boots and a half dozen brood sows and you were in the pig business. America is truly the land of opportunity! Say not?

The hog farms are now gone but it is said that on a hot day in the United Parcel Service parking lot in Secaucus you can still smell pig manure through the pavement!

My Friend, C. Russell Smith

Most of my stories are about real people and events with certain details changed around a bit, and so the tales must be considered fiction. The following is about my late friend, C. Russell Smith and is absolutely true. He was not an AACA member but owned a '68 Chevy and went to many antique car shows.

Russell loved his family, his farm, and his country. He was one of a kind that made America great. He knew what had to be done and he did it... his *own* way. Instead of a 'slow moving vehicle' decal on the back of his 13 foot wide combine he had a sign which said, "If you can't slow down, smile as you go under."

He had lots of adversities in his life, challenges which would have crushed lesser men, but he went on - always knowing what he had to do.

In the spring of the year that he was 12, his family was moving to another farm. He got home from school one afternoon and nobody was home. (A latchkey kid before anybody locked houses.) The farm equipment was gone, but the key was in the '29 Pontiac which was packed full of household goods including grandma's best chinaware.

Russell got in and drove the six miles to the new home place. His mother was absolutely furious, but his father was as proud as could be; he knew he had a son who knew what had to be done, and who did it his own way.

We buried Russell the Friday afternoon before Christmas. The funeral procession backed up three lanes of holiday traffic on Rt. 22 for one half mile in both directions. He got his own way to the very end.

A Model Farm

Eons ago some genius discovered that if he/she (don't say I'm not politically correct) cut and dried luxurious summer grasses, their horses, cattle, sheep, goats, camels, llamas and/or alpacas would not starve in the winter and the family would not have to pull up stakes and wander around hunting for forage. This brainstorm created a whole new set of problems including, but not limited to, extra work in cutting and storing the resulting hay. Inventions of bone, stone and wooden sickles, forks, baskets and sheds occurred and the agricultural revolution was off to a good start with territorial drives and property rights squabbles soon following. Thus, "civilization," as we know it, is related to grass.

Fay's Mother and Aunt were considered to be confirmed old maid school teachers living alone in the big frame farmhouse on the old family homestead. The spinsters drove a 1926 Model T Ford Coupe. Then an amazing thing happened – her mother married an old college friend and moved to Michigan. About two years later other amazing things happened – Fay was born and the stock market crashed after a long bull market. Factories and businesses closed and people lost their jobs or were forced to take pay cuts. Perhaps there is a warning to the "new" economy here – the Dow Jones Average closed at 12,442 today.

The school teacher Auntie was forced to take a pay cut (no tenure then) on a take it or leave it basis, the tenant on their farm stopped paying rent and the new family man in Michigan lost his job. What to do? Frantic phone calls went back and forth and a solution emerged.

The Michigan folks packed up their things and their new baby and headed back East in his brand new Model A Ford just as the "Okies" headed westward. Once they were all settled in the farmhouse, the family took over the farm and cows and relieved the tenant of his lease obligations. They contacted the local county agricultural agent who suggested that they just grow pasture and hay for the cows. The farm did have electricity and they bought milking machines from the local McCormick Deering dealer on time. It was difficult since they knew little about farming and the man of the family was not accustomed to hard physical work. The neighbors were very helpful and by "sharing" work they were able to get the hay crop mowed.

But between cutting hay and putting it away in the barn, several days of nice, sunny, rain-free days are needed. Damp hay put in a hay mow carries the risk of spontaneous combustion and devastating fire. Frey's law (like Murphy's) states that if hay is mowed then it will rain. Rained on hay will rot in the field if it is not fluffed up and aerated. The British call this process wuffling and we call it tedding. So it became necessary to immediately buy a new hay tedder from the local machinery dealer, again on credit.

A tedder of that era was a horse drawn sulky with 8 pitch fork devices driven by a cross mounted crank shaft that threw the hay up in the air and turned it over somewhat. Since they did not own a tractor, the plan was to pull the tedder with the Model T car. The hay tedder's speed could not exceed four miles per hour so it was necessary to hold the left foot pedal down at all times. It didn't take too long to figure out that a 2x4 with a notch and a cleat on it worked fairly well for keeping the T in low but they found the car would boil over in the summer heat even though it was a 1926 high radiator model. So they ended up bolting a scrap piece of angle iron to the almost new Model A Ford's rear bumper and using it as a tractor to get the hay ready and to pull a borrowed hay rake.

When the hay was finally dry the neighbors helped load the loose hay on to wagons and the Model T was put to work getting it into the barn. A man on the top of the load of hay stuck a huge fork into the hay. Fingers on this three foot U-shaped device grabbed a portion of the hay and it was pulled up into the hay mow by the Model T using a system of long ropes and pulleys. The bunch of hay was then released and the Model T returned to its starting point.

So it went throughout the Great Depression, with the family surviving with a large garden, home canned veggies, fruits and meat and some cash income from the milk check for essentials and to pay the taxes. The family relied on their own initiative and labor, help from kindly neighbors (who were in similar straights) and Fay grew up in a loving household surrounded with lots of library books and animal pets and she never knew she was poor.

Love's Old Sweet Song

Once in the dear dead days beyond recall there was a young man with a shiny 1928 orange Chrysler roadster with cream colored wheels. He had purchased it cheap...as it was a gas hog. Gas was expensive (about 10 cents a gallon) and money was in very short supply. His father, however, had a 275 gallon tank of distillate which was used in the International Harvester dual fuel 10-20 farm tractor. Distillate was a cross between modern kerosene and #2 diesel (furnace) oil. It had a higher flash point than gas and sold for 3 cents a gallon bulk delivered. The tractor would be started on gasoline, warmed up, then shifted over to run on distillate. Before stopping the engine it had to be shifted back to gas again, so it would start the next time.

Our "hero," inspired by his father's dual fuel tractor, soon modified his roadster in similar fashion. With distillate in the gas tank and the top down he took a ride every evening and found he had no trouble picking up girls. As a matter of fact, many nights he had a car full of girls and learned what fun girls could be. His buddies had, at best, 10 year old Model "T" Fords, or more likely, took any dates they could get for a ride on the trolley. Therefore, our youth began to see himself as a ladies man since he had little competition. He got up enough nerve to ask a nice young lady whom he always admired for a date, and she accepted.

So they went to the amusement park and rode the merry-go-round. He bought her an ice cream cone. On the way home, with the canvas top down, they stopped to admire the stars, to talk, and to get to know each other better.

When it was time to go home he tried to start his Chrysler, but it would not start!!! The starter ground on and on until the battery died. Alas, he had forgotten to switch to gas before he stopped the engine. Belatedly, he did so and then managed to find the crank under the rumble seat. He cranked and cranked. He sweated and cranked. The hour grew later and she cranked too!

Now it must be remembered that this was well before the "now" generation and girls were expected to be home at night by parents and neighbors. They decided they had better walk the 3 miles to her home. They arrived hand and hand to find both her parents up and wide awake. Her mother had stayed awake remembering what young men had been like.

Now I won't bore you with details of the conversation that ensued but I can say they all lived happily ever after and the family still has that 1928 roadster in the barn!!

A Midsummer's Nightmare

Tommy was thinking, "What could be better than this?" A nice summer evening, a 1950 Olds 88 convertible with the top down and a pretty girl at his side. They cruised up and down Northampton Street and then out in the country onto River Road.

She had her learner's permit (Ah, sweet 16 plus one) and convinced him to let her drive. She did pretty well going past the cottages, but when she went up the grade at the railroad crossing she turned too quickly and the car got stuck on the tracks.

Tommy shoved her out and tried to back up, but the car was really stuck! Bumper to bumper and everything between was resting on and parallel to one rail.

The 10:02 mail train was due pretty soon so Tommy started out on a dead run and left the poor girl wringing her hands and crying. It was a mile and one half to Frey's place, and he arrived completely winded. I got the trusty Model H Farmall tractor, a couple of log chains and with Tommy hanging on, tore down the road and backed up to the car.

With some difficulty we got a chain on the rear axle and with Tommy steering, got the car off the tracks. I can't say it was as close as in the old melodrama movies, but we could feel the evil vibes of that 10:02 in the rails as we hooked up the log chain.

Dear John and the
Great American Dream

John was born well over 100 years ago in one of the middle European countries so often beset by warfare. As a kid he dreamed of America, that great land of opportunity. He worked, scrimped and saved so that at age 17 he came over by boat. He got a job in the coal mines of *central Pennsylvania near (spelled with one L) Philipsburg.* There he learned the language, (including the cuss words), worked hard and saved his money. But he was lonesome and so he went back to the 'old country', a handsome, dapper, worldly wise young man with money in his pockets. He soon made quite a hit with the young peasant girls, but was almost immediately drafted into the Army. By the fortunes of war, he survived as an aide to a General who wanted him to re-enlist at the end of that war, "The war to end all wars." But he wanted no part of that and so he returned to his home town as a war hero.

He courted and soon married a fine young peasant girl and they set out for America. They got off the boat, were processed by authorities, took the ferry to Jersey City and got on the Jersey Central train west. When the conductor yelled "Phillipsburg," they got off. The town looked different, and it was; it was *Phillipsburg, New Jersey!*

Imagine being in a foreign land with a new wife. You hardly speak the language and have barely enough money to get the two of you to the town you've told her about, the town where you might have a few friends, know where to find work, and even have a nice little one-room "honeymoon" apartment reserved for the two of you, and then... you get off *at the wrong train station!* But John, undaunted, searched for and found a job in that strange new town. He and his bride scrimped and saved and they soon bought a small but hilly and rough farm that had a nice little house and barn. They picked rocks and tilled the land, her leading the horse and him handling the plow in the "old world" fashion.

After a few years, the barn on a farm with better land burned down. John and his wife were then able to swap their nice little place for it. They bought a team of horses and my grandmother clucked, "Those dumb foreigners don't even know how to hook up a team of horses!" But my grandfather made friends with John, who learned fast. Through hard work they built a new barn, fixed up the old stone farmhouse and raised a family and bountiful crops.

In 1939, they bought a styled flywheel start John Deere "B" tractor with #4B (two bottom) plow and cultivators. He learned to drive it and would be out slowly cultivating corn (with shields) when it only had 2 leaves. He carried a hoe on the tractor and if he knocked over a plant he would set it back up or plant another seed. He was a true steward of the land and there wasn't a weed or varmint allowed on the place. After Mass on Sunday he would get on his Model B (he never drove a car) and check out all of his fields (and his neighbors', too).

John died a few years ago, after he fell out of the haymow, but his bride is still alive...she will be 100 years old this fall! Five generations live on the farm today and it's the nicest, neatest place you'll find anywhere.

The interstate runs near their farm and every day thousands of commuters in their Japanese cars buzz by in search of the "great American dream." What they don't understand is that it still exists and they've just rushed past it. What a great country this is!

Harry H. Frey sits proudly on his new 1946 Farmall H tractor which was destined for export to Russia. The tractor had a wider-than-normal 100 inch long rear axles, as it was manufactured to fit the wider crop rows of that country. Setting the wheels the appropriate distance for American crops meant the axles protruded beyond the tires. After hitting his crotch all too often, he got a handful of hacksaw blades and sawed off the three-inch tempered steel *by hand.*

Hike!

Not only does the Lehigh Valley boast of an active antique car club, but it has acquired the Philadelphia Eagles' Training Camp. Summer used to be for baseball and to me it is just too hot for football. Of course the professional athletes work out in air conditioned weight rooms. Even some high schools now have air conditioned weight rooms where the aspiring jocks can "bulk up" in total comfort. Talk about an affluent society!

It didn't used to be that way. If a farmer needed some strong high school boys to haul and unload hay, all he had to do was call coach "Whiz", and the heroes would show up and work hard. If they didn't, they were off the team because "Whiz" was a no-nonsense football coach.

But "Whiz" almost did not get involved in football. His parents did not want their handsome son to play football at all. In 1919 about all the protection a high school player had was a leather helmet and the Rhineharts were worried that he would get crippled up with bad knees.

Like all young men, "Whiz" wanted a car and so the family got him to promise not to go out for the team and they would buy him a car. They gave him a robin's egg blue Essex Roadster for his birthday, but when football season came around young "Whiz" forgot his promise and secretly used the roadster to get himself and teammates to and from practice. After the first game, his mother was absolutely furious, but his father was downright proud. Although nobody knew how, Papa eventually got Mama cooled down.

"Whiz" went on to star in football at Lafayette College where he later taught and coached. But for forty years he taught physics and coached his winning high school football team. He eventually married (at age 45) a high school classmate and lived a quiet and dignified country life raising standardbred horses...and his knees held up until he was 90.

Willard "Whiz" Rhinehart died last fall at age 92 and is remembered by some as the old guy with the border collies in the back of his pickup truck. But to many he is recalled as the coach who made men out of boys, and was a mentor and advisor to many. But nearly everybody has forgotten about his robin's egg blue Essex and his promise.

P.S: One of the most famous of "Whiz's" boys was Jim Ringo. This lanky kid went out for high school football and "Whiz" found out the youth could pass the ball backward thru his legs with his head upside down about as well as most guys could throw a forward pass. You see, in the days before Knute Rockne's "T" formation, it was extremely important for the center to get the ball to whichever backfield man was to carry the pigskin. Thus, a star was made. Jim Ringo dominated the game as a center with Vince Lombardi's Green Bay Packers in the late 1950's and is a National Football Hall of Fame athlete.

Foggy February

February is the month of fog, thaws, freshets... and skunks. Like the proverbial groundhogs they come out of their holes but are more noticeable. Almost anyone who has spent much time outdoors has a skunk story. My son, Rob, at age eleven, shot one, picked it up by the tail to show Mama and immediately realized his mistake!

The Boyers had money—old money going back to a land grant from the King of England in the 1700's—and nobody ever spent much of it. For generations the farms had been rented out to share croppers. It was an honor to farm a fertile Boyer place, and both tenants and landlords prospered. Eventually the smart boys at the Internal Revenue Service figured out that dead folks couldn't complain and instituted inheritance tax. As each member of the Boyer family died, wills were read, appraisals were made and inheritance taxes paid. My boyhood friend, Donald, was the last heir and he and his wife decided that there wouldn't be any inheritance taxes due when they got done with it.

For starters, they dined out every evening and bought a pair of matching Mercedes. The original family mansion had been sold off in 1902, and they repurchased it. They had the stone work sandblasted and repointed and all twelve rooms professionally restored and decorated. They put on a new slate roof and had the grounds landscaped. When everything was absolutely perfect they held an open house and invited my wife and me.

We arrived on this foggy February night to find the lane parked full of Cadillacs, Lincolns, BMWs, Jaguars and even a nice Bentley. Obviously, this was going to be a high class event – so we went to the back door, through the pantry into the kitchen and hung up our coats in the servant's quarters. We eased our way into the main hall where the buffet was set up on the solid cherry table with about twelve leaves in it. And such food it was – rich and exotic and in unbelievable quantities. We filled our plates, made some small talk and headed for a corner where we wouldn't spill anything on the oriental rugs.

It really was quite a party! Anybody who was anybody was there... the former Governor, the head of the Republican Committee, D.A.R. Ladies, and all the bank directors. The rooms were full of well-dressed folks, many of whom were clustered around the old pantry – now a bar. Donald, the ever gracious host, introduced us to several people as we refilled our plates a second time and began to feel a bit more at ease. I found a group of elegantly dressed ladies at the top of the grand staircase waiting to use the bathroom, and being a country boy I decided to go outside. I went past the old carriage house—now a garage—and out of sight behind the corn crib. I started to relieve myself and looked down to see a pair of small beady eyes looking up at me, as if to ask why it suddenly had started to rain warm rain. A SKUNK!

What happened? Well, I'll let you be the judge and figure out how it all ended, but like I said earlier it was quite a party!!!

My Dad

He was a good man. Far better than I, and I figured this out at an early age. He was religious and sang in the church choir for 70 years with a clear strong baritone voice. He was a good mechanic, a patient man, and I never once heard him swear. He was a farmer and farmers have a lot to cuss about. But he never once did. He did mutter sometimes under his breath and with me around he had a reason to do so. He and I worked together almost daily for forty years (with and for each other). I miss him and his advice although at times I must admit I did not relish or welcome his advice. Looking back on it now I guess he was usually right and I'd like to share this story about what an all right guy he was.

Things were scarce on the home front during World War II. On the farm we had plenty of food and could get gasoline for the tractor but my father never put a drop of it in the car. He had an 'A' ration stamp for the car and bought his allotment at the local gas station. About the only place we went was to Old Greenwich Church. Dad's car tires were poor and he 'made do' with second hand recaps and blow out patches.

The lang and bolster broke on dad's hay wagon so he went to the Ration Board and got approval to buy a whole new farm wagon running gear. He ordered it from the Sears Roebuck catalog and when it came by Railway Express it had four brand new B.F. Goodrich passenger car tires mounted on the wheels. Nobody had seen new car tires for over three years, but my father put them on his hay wagon and there they stayed.

Our neighbor Ken's 1937 Chevy car needed tires also. When he heard about my father's wagon tires, he got Ration Board approval and immediately ordered a Sears wagon. But his came with ribbed 6.00 x 16 front tractor tires (see picture) which he promptly put on his car and went off to Atlantic City. My dad thought it was totally improper to do such a thing and I thought my dad was kind of stupid to leave new tires on a hay wagon. But now I know my father was a man Diogenes was looking for and I'm proud to be his son. If your dad is still around be sure to give him a hug next Father's Day.

Harry H. Frey & Son

My Mom

My mother, Marian Hance Frey, was born in 1903, married during the Great Depression and had me in 1931.

She was a working mother if there ever was one, but she worked at home and on the farm: cooking, cleaning, washing (Maytag putt-putt-putt), ironing and canning produce from her garden. You haven't really eaten well unless you have tasted home canned pork chops - and pies made from canned elderberries. She also fed the calves, carried milk from barn to milk house and scrubbed up the milking machines daily for years.

Her pin money was the egg money. Every March she got two hundred baby chicks (by U.S. mail) and raised them on home grown grains that my father ground with his John Deere tractor and Letz feed mill. The roosters were eaten or sold as broilers and the hens were kept for the eggs. These mother gathered, candled, graded, sorted and then delivered to her customers in town every Friday.

Sometimes folks only needed (or could only afford) six eggs, but mother always sold all of her eggs or she traded them for groceries at the A & P Store.

One warm spring day in 1941, she was coming down Stockton Street hill and forced to slam on the brakes to miss a kid on a bicycle and thus dumped three big (Longaberger style) egg baskets off the back seat and on the floor of the 1931 Chevrolet two-door.

Marian Frey & Son
(Note the bib overalls.)

31

My mother was a happy, bright and intuitive person but this really spoiled her day and week. She went home, called all of her egg customers on the phone and apologized for the inconvenience. She then got the water hose and started to flush the omelet out of the car. The resulting mess ran under the front seats and out on the running boards and stuck fast. She tried everything she could think of — Fels Naptha, Rinso, Oxydol and even Lysol. My father came in from the fields and being the Christian gentleman he was, told her it was all right — she had not hit the bicyclist and just not to worry.

But it wasn't all right. As summer came on so did the flies. Maggots grew in the joints where the fenders joined the running boards. By the time the really hot days of August arrived the car smelled like sulfur dioxide and flies crawled all over the garage like they did when mother cooked sauerkraut in the kitchen.

Clearly something had to be done so my father bought an almost new 1941 two tone green Chevrolet Special Deluxe Sedan from a young man who had enlisted in the Marines. World War II soon broke out and the Frey family had a "new" car for five whole years. The 1931 Chevy was readily sold (smell and all) and was occasionally seen up until VJ Day in 1945. Oh, yes, mother always carried her egg baskets in the trunk of the car henceforth.

Harry Frey hosing off the 1931 Chevrolet

Smokey and the Bandit Hunter

Smokey lived and breathed, ate and slept deer hunting. He knew who had shot every single deer, anywhere in the township over the past twenty years. He knew the spot it was shot, how big it was, who else had shot at it, and most importantly, the size of the rack and the number of points.

Smokey was the first hunter to bag a deer every year and would have one hanging up in his big oak tree almost as soon as the season opened. He spent a lot of time prowling the fields and woods.

One cold dark night while Smokey was riding around in his pickup truck, he saw a spotlight beam coming from a 1954 red Jeep station wagon in my hay field. "Those damn deer jackers," he muttered as he drove across the field after them. The Jeep started up, headed for the dirt lane, went down the township road, and turned left on the county road with Smokey in hot pursuit. The Jeep turned into George's field and with its four-wheel drive went bumpty bump across the corn rows with the lights out. Smokey couldn't keep up and lost sight of the Jeep, so he went home to bed. He'd had enough excitement for one night and a story to tell his deer hunting buddies the next day.

What Smokey didn't know (or claims he didn't know) was that the Jeep got to the fence row, took a right turn and where there was an opening in the tree line, turned left and disappeared over a cliff.

The cement company had abandoned operations years ago when they hit a vein of water which they could not pump down. This quarry had sixty feet of water in it, and it was a good eighty foot drop down a vertical cliff to the water level.

About thirty feet down from the edge there was a lone tree growing out of a crack in the limestone. On this wild cherry tree that Jeep landed on its side and balanced there.

The next morning Mrs. Kosack was out walking her dog and heard a man cry "HELP!". Police, emergency squad, fire department, water rescue team and several wreckers were called. It was a mighty cold, bruised poacher that was eventually rescued. They say he never went hunting again... BUT Smokey does, and that's the honest truth.

PS: Smokey got arrested this fall by a Dept. of Fish and Wildlife officer.

Sweet Violet

"Sweet Violet, sweeter than the roses" was an old song and it described Violet as a young bride. Bob courted her in his Model A Ford. She was six years younger than he, just a pretty kid who had never learned to drive. She married the tall handsome young man and they moved into the old stone farmhouse with the in-laws --- a tenuous situation at best. But she was up to the challenge and held her own with her mother-in-law. She helped in the house and in the barn and had her very own garden.

When the men were making hay and needed all the help they could get, Bob asked Violet if she would rake the hay. It was easy, he would show her how to drive the tractor and she could get a nice tan. He rode on the fender of the 9N Ford for three or four rounds until she understood how to operate the tractor and rake. When he was confident she knew what she was doing he left her to do the raking. Off she went in second gear, one third throttle, nice and slow around and around with the tractor straddling the swath with the John Deere side delivery rake rolling up nice big windrows. The corners were not too square, but all in all, by the end of the haying season she was a pretty confident tractor driver. During some pillow talk Bob promised her he would teach her to drive a car.

Thanks to Violet the men finished up the hay-making one day earlier than they had other years, and everybody was happy. Bob asked Violet to take the tractor and steel wheeled rake down to the barn. He threw the rake out of gear and raised it up so that the tines would not drag and admonished Violet to GO SLOW – "use third gear with the throttle closed and use the brakes so you don't go too fast" he said. It was about one third of a mile to the barn, downhill all the way and the gradient became steeper the closer she got to the buildings. The rear wheels on the hay rake began to shimmy so Violet decided to apply the brakes.

Here it must be explained that Ford 9N tractors came out in 1939 and in many ways were far ahead of both the competition and the times. Henry Ford and Harry Ferguson had done a good job collaborating on the overall design and with the hydraulic lift system in particular. But there was a problem with the controls. The right brake pedal controlled the right rear brake and was designed to assist in turning right. There was a similar pedal on the left side adjacent to and level with the clutch pedal. This one was to help turn left.

Violet pushed on the right brake pedal and she simultaneously pushed on the clutch pedal (instead of the left brake), which effectively threw the little Ford tractor out of gear. The right drive wheel locked up and slid on the gravel road as Violet mistakenly stood on the clutch as hard as she could. The differential gears allowed her to go faster and faster – maybe twenty miles an hour or more.

Violet rode it out, steered as best she could down the hill, turned left into the driveway, missing the fence posts, milk house, barnyard wall, corn crib, wagon house and came to a stop in her mother-in-law's potato patch.

Violet decided, right then and there, that she was never going to drive a motor vehicle again. No tractors. Not even a car.
And she never did.

The hill Violet unintentionally raced down on a Ford 9N tractor.
Circa 1950's

M'm, M'm, Good!

In America today tomatoes are available year round. In Winter they are strip mined down in Texas, sorted electronically at 20 per second, shrink wrapped on Styrofoam and sent north with all the taste and consistency of raw potatoes. Along the middle of February I'd give anything for a nice soft "Big Boy" tomato. Just the kind you'd love to throw at the neighbor's cat --- if only you could get a good grip on it. Did you ever wonder what happens to all those soft squishy tomatoes every summer?

Years ago Campbell's had a big cannery in Camden, NJ. Baskets of dead ripe tomatoes came in by the truckload to be processed into Campbell's soup. (The Campbell Kid wasn't smiling in those old ads -- he was smirking).

Farmers would contract with Campbell's and when the tomatoes were ripe would go to the poor section of town in the cool early morning, knock on doors and ask if anybody wanted to work. This was before the Great Society with unemployment compensation, relief payments, food stamps and aid to dependent children. It was always possible to get a pickup truck load of eager workers. Seventeen cents a basket was pretty good money then and despite the fact some of the workers did not show up the next day, the word was out and somebody else was always willing to work. The one half bushel baskets were loaded on flatbed stake body trucks and stacked so that the bottom of the baskets rested on the top rim of the previous layer.

"Jay" hauled tomatoes for a produce trucking company. Campbell's did have their limits, however, and refused his load as being just too soft and squishy. Jay called his boss who said to take the load over to Palm, PA where there was a processor that would take anything.

Just as Jay got the 1951 Ford F-6 truck up to the toll booth of the Tacony-Palmyra Bridge the traffic was halted when the draw bridge rose to allow a ship to pass up the Delaware River. When Jay stopped, the fruit flies caught up to his truck. They filled Jay's cab, they filled the toll booths, they called in reinforcements from Camden County so that there were fruit flies everywhere as the truck sat oozing tomato juice in the boiling hot sun.

The bridge cops abandoned their toll booths, surrounded and started examining the stake body truck. When the drawbridge finally came down and Jay paid his toll, one of the police said to Jay, "If you _ever_ come through here again, we're going to impound your truck!!"

It's the honest truth -- or so Jay told me.

The Yellow and the White Stuff

No, you dirty old men, I'm not writing about the yellow snow, I'm writing about the yellow caution lights. This time of year commuters start to fuss if it snows three flakes to the acre. They hurry home to toss and turn and worry about how to get back to work the next day.

"Indy" was the original commuter. He had worked at a Fort Wayne facility during World War II. After that he worked as a traveling salesman or at various jobs, none of which were close to home. He'd tear off at 6 a.m. at 65 m.p.h. and stop somewhere for coffee and not get back until 7 p.m. Then after supper he might go out to the Esso Station so he could get a good start in the morning.

Since he had worked in the Studebaker factory he drove Land Cruisers and Diplomats and had the first Studebaker Hawk that I ever saw (it was bright John Deere green and yellow). He was faithful to the end with a Canadian Chevy powered Lark and then one of the Studebaker Packards (or Packard Studebakers).

When Studebaker closed he went to hemihead Chryslers and continued on with fast and usually expensive cars.

He took the Mrs. to all the Policemen's Balls, donated to all the police benevolent associations and had lots of police booster stickers and chrome stars in his rear window. He dutifully transferred these to each new car.

The only trouble was that of the thirty cars he owned in his lifetime, he totaled a total of thirteen and they all were mostly just plain open hearth material.

"Indy" retired at age 72 and bought a BMW. He still managed to find places to go; Lenhartsville for that good smoked sausage, Scranton to get his favorite cigars, Metuchen to an all-night pharmacy for his pills.

So it came to pass that he was traveling through Phillipsburg on Route 22 when the traffic light at Roseberry Street turned to yellow. The car in front of him stopped - but "Indy" didn't. He got out of his car and indignantly shouted to the lady he had rear ended, "If you hadn't stopped for that yellow light, we could have both made it through!!"

Buried Treasure

Anyone who reads old car magazines is familiar with the story: someone finds an antique car hidden away in a garage or old barn. The car hasn't seen daylight in years, but the forsaken vehicle is miraculously resurrected. Its proud new owner lovingly restores it to its former glory.

I recently got involved in the rediscovery of a 1918 Model T Ford "huckster" truck. I had heard about its existence for years and got a call from Hank who was considering selling it to an acquaintance (we will call) Ben. The Ford was in Hank's late uncle's two story frame blacksmith's shop. The structure had been placed on the National Historic Registry and had a plaque to prove it. Actually the whole town had been placed on the Historic Registry in a futile attempt to stop the big box super store from coming in.

The key fit the lock and the door creaked open and we peered into the blackness. It soon became obvious that we had to remove parts of a forty-foot extension ladder to get inside. Then we were confronted by boxes of glass Mason jars, Planet Junior garden tools, boxes, chicken crates, a crumbling forge, anvils, hammers, fishing rods, eel gigs, piles of empty potato sacks and stuff even I did not recognize. All of this detritus of several lifetimes was once somebody's treasure and we had to climb over and through it.

Ben (who, though far from young, was the youngest) scrambled over the junk, armed with an aerosol bomb of WD-40 and sprayed the hood latches, hood hinges, and door hinges. (WD-40 also chases mud wasps away.) Hank and I carefully picked our way through the gloom. The Model T had a decided list to the left and Ben found out why, as the floor boards gave way beneath his feet and he fell through the floor to his shins. Fortunately, he was not hurt.

As we examined the truck, Hank related its history to us. It was purchased new by the town fire company as a ladder truck and was equipped with a Ruckstell two-speed rear. Some of the gilded lettering still showed through the dust. Eventually Hank's uncle bought it and used it as a "huckster truck" to deliver home-grown produce to town. Every Saturday morning he would pick up Hank and head for the city, where Hank would go door to door with a basket of vegetables and ask each housewife if she needed anything. When he finally sold all the produce, Hank's uncle would stop at a tiny restaurant and buy the boy a ham and cheese sandwich and a five-cent bottle of soda pop.

The hood and doors opened easily but the engine was stuck tight. Standing on the crank handle only threatened to bend the crank. So we sprayed the spark plug holes with WD-40 and reluctantly left the Model T where it was so Ben could think about whether it would make a good rolling billboard for his small family business.

We picked our way back through the junk, put the extension ladders back inside and locked up the building. We all decided it would take three or four guys at least three full days just to get the Model T into the daylight. There was some doubt as to whether Ben really wanted to buy the truck. There was even more doubt as to whether Hank was really going to sell it.

Personally, I don't think he'll ever part with it. I know how Hank is. If you are the kind of person who never gets rid anything, a person whose parents and grandparents never got rid of anything – then it is nearly impossible to part with a treasure such as a Model T. The "huckster truck" is rusted and rotted. It hasn't moved for decades. It is covered with dust and mouse droppings. But to this day, it still delivers something. It carries a young boy's memories to a weathered, (but still moving) old man.

The Pumpkin Flood

"You get in the boat first," Art said to his wife, Mary Francis. "I'll hand the baby to you and then I'll get in." Their neighbor, Mr. Rapp, had rowed out in the swiftly-rising muddy water to rescue the young family from the second story of their half-submerged home. Mary Francis and Art had been married only a year and a half when they had rented this farm along the Delaware River. The barn was up on the hill so the animals were safe, but the crops and the wood-framed house were in the bottomland.

As the flood waters filled the first floor of their home, they had hurriedly moved the few belongings they possessed up the central stairway to the second floor. Now, kneeling on the front porch roof and holding onto the bow of the rowboat with one hand, Art (who could not swim) handed the child to his wife, breathed a prayer and scrambled in beside them.

Mr. Rapp rowed back to the nearest high ground, which was the Bel-Del Railroad right of way. Mrs. Rapp said that the family could stay with them until the water receded.

The next day Mary Francis and Art solemnly surveyed the damage. Plaster was falling off the laths. Mud covered every stair step. The cook stove dripped water. Floorboards had buckled. The rug was a soggy mess. Outside, the privy had toppled and the hole posed a stinking danger. (In fact, *everything* stunk!) Logs and sawed lumber from the nearby sawmill littered the yard. And amazingly, (as though a colorful touch of humor was needed in this disaster,) there were bright orange pumpkins everywhere! Pumpkins rested unnaturally in the bushes. Pumpkins floated in Art's half-submerged corn field. Pumpkins decorated the inside of the otherwise mud-filled house. Somebody upstream was missing a lot of them.

Renting this farm had seemed like such a good idea. The house was decent and the rent fair. The landlord was honest and it was a chance for the young couple to start out on their own. Art also could grind his cow feed when the waterpower was not needed to run the sawmill. Mary Francis had enthusiastically papered the downstairs and fixed up a room for the baby upstairs. Now she had even lost her garden. A whole years work for nothing and they had no money. Their savings had gone into purchasing field equipment and fixing up the house. They were penniless and distraught. All they had now were the cows, the horses and a flotilla of pumpkins.

Since there was no other alternative, they moved in with Art's parents. Two men on the same farm and two women in the same kitchen: it was not the ideal arrangement. But they made the best of it. It worked for ten years – living together in a narrow grey farmhouse - until Mary Francis and Art could afford to build their own home: a brick two-story "American Four-square."

Actually the family arrangement has worked for over one hundred years - six generations. The house that was flooded burned down about twenty years ago just west of the iron railroad bridge on River Road, Pohatcong Township, NJ. My wife and I live in that "American Four-square" that my grandparents built up on a hill, a mile from the Delaware. And, oh yes, that infant rescued from the second story during the 1903 "Pumpkin Flood" was my father, Harry H. Frey.

Flood of 2004 – View of site where tenant house used to stand.

Flood of 2004 - deluged soybean field where corn grew in 1903.

Cabbage Patch Roll

Hawky often bragged as to how quickly he could take his six cans of milk to the creamery on Sunday mornings. Sundays were special – the Sabbath, a day of rest, but it took a lot of hurrying around in order to be able to get away from the farm for five or six hours. He had to feed and milk his cows, load the 40 quart (2 pints to a quart and a pint is a pound) milk cans in the back of his Model A Ford pickup, grab a scrambled egg sandwich and head for town.

This particular late fall Sunday the plans were to go to Sunday School and then head up to Tranquility (there really is a town by that name) to visit his wife's aunt, Edith.   A good Sunday dinner and delightful conversation was sure to follow as everybody shared the happenings in their (and other's) lives.

Hawky was thinking about what he was going to tell those folks, and about what good time he was making this day on his way to the creamery. His record was 27 minutes for the 12 mile round trip including unloading the milk cans and waiting for the steam-sterilizer to wash the empty cans. He was pushing the Model A pretty hard as he came to a tee in the road with a lot of wet leaves in the intersection. Model A brakes were pretty good for slowing down, but not much good for stopping when the brake rods get stretched and his sagged quite a lot.

He couldn't stop.   He went right through the intersection into Mrs. Josack's cabbage patch, straddling a row as the front axle rolled the cabbages out by the roots. Hawky made a U-turn in the muddy patch and then bounced over the dirt mounds where the old lady had buried her salsify and winter-keeper beets.   This, of course, upset some of the milk cans and sent milk and can lids flying. Mrs. Josack heard this commotion as she sat in her outhouse. She sprang to her feet, grabbed a hoe that was standing in the comer of the privy, and headed in Hawky's direction as fast as her old legs would carry her.

He picked up his milk can lids, jumped back in the Model A and raced toward town with Mrs. Josack brandishing her hoe and cursing in her native Russian. Hawkey didn't beat his 27 minute record that day, but he surely did have a good story to tell later at Aunt Edith's.

DeSoto Saga: Part 1
June 2001

Almost every issue of our national AACA magazine has a story about someone who finds a dusty antique car in some decrepit barn and pesters the owner, an old farmer in bib-overalls and a John Deere cap, until he finally agrees to sell. Then the hero of the story restores the car to its former glory.

My story is somewhat different because in this case, I am the old farmer.

Fifty years ago, my wife's parents had a 1937 DeSoto which they used solely to go shopping and a very occasional trip to the Jersey Shore. By 1950, my (eventual) mother-in-law decided that they needed a new car and started pestering her husband about it. Finally he picked up the phone and called nearby Burholm Motors and told them to bring over a new car. And just like that, they bought it! No comparative shopping. No tire kicking. Some people just hate to shop. They had the "new" car for twenty years and only put thirty thousand miles on it with her riding in the back seat like Miss Daisy. Eventually, my father-in-law had a fender-bender and it became apparent that he should no longer drive. So it became my sad duty to remove the rotor from the distributor – knowing full well that someday the same thing would probably happen to me.

When my father-in-law passed away the family gave the DeSoto to me, and I used it as an "errand" car around the farm for a couple of years until it dawned on me that I should really take better care of it. So I changed the oil, parked it in the barn, and kept my eyes open for NOS chrome at antique car meets such as Hershey.

Two summers ago, my wife's nephew, Charles, visited us and discovered his grandfather's old car hiding in our barn, covered with dust and bird droppings. He recalled riding in it as a kid and mentioned that he would like to have it and would fix it up. I immediately said, "Good! It's yours! And furthermore, I will deliver it!" I knew I would never get around to restoring it, and the old car deserved a second chance. I loaded it onto a trailer, and hauled it from New Jersey to North Carolina.

To be continued.....

DeSoto Saga: Part 2
April 2002

Someone asked me about the restoration of my father-in-law's 1950 DeSoto. His grandson, Charles, after much internet searching, located a badly needed new-old stock gasoline tank and paid through the nose. While trailering the car to a well-known Alabama restoration shop, Charles passed another 1950 DeSoto with a "for sale" sign on it. Twenty miles down the road he decided to go back and buy it for a parts car.

It had a clock and a radio! Grandpa was too tight to buy a "loaded" car back in 1950. As a matter of fact, he would not even run the heater for fear of running down the battery! The parts car also had a good gas tank (no longer required) and a badly needed set of inside running boards.

As of this writing, my father-in-law's car has been stripped and phosphate coated. It still needs upholstery, paint, and the overhauled engine installed.

Hopefully, it will be ready in time to surprise the rest of the family at the wedding of Charles's niece. But as most car enthusiasts have found out, restoration always takes a lot more time and money than anticipated.

To be continued...

DeSoto Saga: Part 3
March 2003

We trailered my father-in-law's 1950 DeSoto to my wife's nephew in Charlotte, NC in June of 2000. We unloaded it at a neighborhood brake shop that promised to "get right on it." It took over four months to get the car drivable.

Charles learned how to surf the net for parts. It took months to accumulate all the pieces, adding them to the pile of new old stock chrome I had gathered over the last 20 years at the Hershey antique car swap meets. DeSoto chrome looks deceptively like Dodge and Chrysler stuff but it just won't fit!

Finally the restoration man got a Corvette out of his one-man shop and Charles was able to get his grandfather's car to take its place in August, 2001. It took three trips to get all the pieces to a dip and strip place and everything was immediately primed. The motor was shipped out to an experienced machine shop even though it had only 37,000 miles on it and it had 40 pounds of oil pressure.

Charles wanted everything perfect. After all, he had known the car well. As a kid, when the family came to visit the grandparents every summer in Philadelphia, Grandma paid Charles to polish it. His grandfather, a careful man, always blew the horn at every intersection. He rode with the window down so he could give hand signals in addition to the turn signals. He never let the tank drop below half-full and never let Charles ride in the front seat. The boy dreamed of driving it himself, someday.

The restoration man painted everything inside and out with the body, fenders and hood all off the frame. It was done in modern paint to the exact, original, pale blue. The rebuilt six-cylinder was painted silver and returned with the rebuilt radiator. It took eight men to set the body back on the frame. The hood took a long time to get fit correctly. The freshly plated chrome was fitted with utmost care. Beautiful. A truly perfect job.

Charles had found the correct upholstery material after a lengthy internet search and had it shipped from Washington state. The DeSoto, almost finished, was taken to a highly recommended upholstery man to complete the restoration. He promised to have the work all done in plenty of time for Charles to drive it to his niece's upcoming wedding. The grand old car had been the bride's great-grandfather's and it was Charles's idea to have it be a big surprise for the attending relatives - as the bridal car.

But when Charles went to pick up the big, blue, shining DeSoto from the upholsterer, he took one look at it and felt sick --- absolutely ill.

To be continued…

DeSoto Saga: Part 4
March 2003

One year and nine months after I had trailered his grandfather's 1950 DeSoto to North Carolina, Charles got the call from the upholsterer that the car was all finished. He rushed to the shop, but for some reason the upholstery man did not greet Charles at the door as usual.

When Charles looked at the car he was sick – sick at heart. The roof had five cones of stretched metal near the window molding! Zits on an otherwise flawless beauty!

Mr. Upholstery said it wasn't his fault. He said it was Charles's fault for providing the wrong length screws for the interior molding. The restoration man said it would be very hard to fix and he wasn't even sure if he had any more of the special DeSoto robin's-egg-blue paint remaining.

Charles had a real dilemma. He had promised to provide the wedding car for his niece's upcoming wedding, and the wedding date was fast approaching. Could it be finished in time? And how much more would it cost? He had already spent enough on his grandfather's DeSoto to have bought a brand new Mercedes.

It took one month and fifteen hundred dollars more to repair the damage. Charles proudly trailered the beautifully restored car to Memphis and hid it in the garage of a neighbor of the mother of the bride. On the day of the wedding, Charles's parents saw it for the first time in twenty-five years and his mother broke down in tears. Flashbulb's flashed. Video cameras rolled. Bridesmaids smiled as Charles's parents got into the heirloom DeSoto. They admired the beautifully upholstered interior.

Charles turned the key. The car did not start. He turned the key again, and again. The refurbished engine refused to respond. Would the bride's grandparents make it to the wedding on time and more importantly… would the great-grandparent's DeSoto?

To be continued…

A comment about the picture on the following page:
Taylor Grocery serves the best fried catfish in the South. Note the sign behind the car trunk. It says, "Eat here, or we both starve."

DeSoto Saga: Part 5
April 2003

The day of the big wedding arrived after months of preparation. Actually, it was *years* if you include the time it took for the 1950 DeSoto's restoration. Cameras recorded the bride's grandparents getting into the car with Charles and his wife up front. Charles turned the ignition key and the car would not start.

Charles's brother, Peter (in tuxedo) and Charles's teenage son, Chase, seized the moment and started pushing. They were able to get the four-thousand pound car coasting down a convenient hill, but there was no tuning over the recently overhauled engine. Panic set in. The mother of the bride started yelling, "Get on the bus! Get on the bus!" The bridesmaids gathered up their long skirts and headed for the antique London double-decker bus which the family had rented in lieu of limos.

Son Chase trotted down the hill to the spot where the car stopped rolling and said, "Dad, open the hood." Despondent Charles said, "It's no use. You can't fix it. You don't know anything about DeSotos."

"Open the hood!" said Chase. At some point, the son becomes father to the man and Charles did open the hood. Chase poked around the engine and found a wire that had jiggered loose while the car was being trailered. Thankfully, Chase was a bit of a teenage motor-head, having fixed up a Landcruiser FJ40, and the straight-six Toyota of the 1970's is basically a 1940's design. "Whoopee!" It started. The original owner's great-grandson had saved the day!

The wedding was a big success, but believe me, not a grain of rice was thrown at – nor were tin cans tied to the back of – the blue DeSoto getaway car!

To be continued… (It ain't over yet, y'all.)

DeSoto Saga: Part 6
August 2003

Charles had borrowed a car trailer to haul the DeSoto and after the big fat southern "you all" wedding in Collegeville, Tennessee, they loaded it up again and headed for Oxford, Mississippi. Chase, the teenage motor-head son, went on ahead with his mother in the SUV. College-age daughter, Laura rode with her dad in the pickup with the 1950 car in tow. DeSotos weigh about two tons. All was going well until a tire blew out on the trailer.

They soon found a gas station and it had a tire that fit. Off they rode again, marveling at how lucky they were to find a replacement – and then, "BANG," another tire blew.

This time they were not so lucky. No exits. No tire stores. No jack. No tools. Charles knew he could not leave the trailer and the car along the interstate. He also knew he could not continue on only three tires.

He decided to unload the DeSoto. (Notice I didn't use the yuppie word "off-load.") Charles would then drive the DeSoto and Laura would follow behind with the pickup and the empty trailer. So off they went with the DeSoto cruising at fifty miles per hour and a pretty girl driving a pickup towing an empty trailer with one tire flapping itself to pieces. What a great CB conversation piece for the trailer truck drivers! Passing motorists flashed their lights, yelled out of rolled-down windows, and tried to flag them down. But they went on, stopping at town after town, trying to find a tire of the correct size.

They came to a bridge over the Tennessee River where the highway narrows down to two lanes. It is a high, steel-girder bridge with a long, steep approach. Charles, in the DeSoto, shifted the "tip-toe" shift down a notch and the Fluid Drive churned away at thirty miles per hour. Trailer trucks behind them lost momentum; their drivers down-shifted and swore profusely as poor Laura, who had hardly ever driven a pickup and who had never driven a trailer (especially a wide one with a flat tire) struggled to maintain her composure. She hoped things will be better once they crested the arch in the center of the bridge and headed down the long slope on the other side.

But the disintegrating tire had wiped out the wires to the electric trailer brakes. With the trailer now pushing her downhill, Laura rode the truck brakes really hard to keep from running over her dad. He, in turn, had to floor the DeSoto to stay ahead of her, not knowing why she kept nosing right up to his bumper.

By the time they found a Firestone store, Charles and Laura were both nervous wrecks. They reloaded the DeSoto and managed to get to their destination safely. The trailer owner wanted (in addition to payment for rewiring the brakes,) two new Michelins to match the original tires on the trailer.

Charles completed a beautiful restoration of his grandfather's DeSoto just in time for his niece's wedding. What joy the sight of the grand old car brought to his parents and siblings! But in the process he learned that car restorations – and weddings - can be expensive and traumatic affairs.

Laura's own wedding was a lovely outdoor ceremony, held on a beautiful June day in 2011. There was, however, no sign of her great-grandfather's 1950 DeSoto.

Moonlit

He wasn't the sharpest knife in the drawer, but Floyd had a job pumping gas. He actually pumped it by hand up into a glass cylinder so that the customer could see how much gas he received. Floyd was glad for the job since it was in the middle of the Great Depression.

One day a gentleman came into the station with a late model International 1½ ton stake-body truck and bought a set of fog lights and had Floyd install them. He set to work with a brace and bit and when the bit got dull he resharpened it on the foot powered grindstone back behind the gas station and continued to drill through the heavy iron bumper. All the while Floyd "scoped out" the truck with its shiny, dark green paint, red wheels, wooden tool box and big extra gas tank under the bed, both properly locked. Boy, he would love to drive a truck like that. He mounted the lights, hooked up the wiring and aimed them. He did a nice job. The truck's owner, Mr. Schantz, was impressed and tipped him. He then asked Floyd if he wanted a part time job a couple of nights a month - *if* he could drive a truck (i.e. double clutch). Synchromesh transmissions were available by 1930 in Buicks and Cadillac cars but were a long time coming to trucks. Floyd, of course, jumped at the chance.

A couple of weeks later he went with Mr. Schantz on a fall evening to deliver a load of baled hay. They went to Trenton to the race track and Mr. Schantz gave Floyd a quarter and sent him across the street to an all-night diner while he talked to some men all dressed up in business suits and fedoras. When Floyd came back from his coffee and pie, Mr. Schantz said, "Ok, now we go to the Freehold race track."

Once there, Floyd was sent down the street for more coffee while a crew of men unloaded the truck. Then, back to Trenton with a sealed envelope and more discussion with the men at the track - and then home, with Floyd driving.

Mr. Schantz had a very nice farm with the house and buildings all painted-up and flowers growing nine months of the year. The fields were well cultivated; the cows and horses were always "all spiffed up." This in contrast to his brother Nick's place down the road which was over-grown with weeds and generally a mess. Mr. Schantz also had a big International 15-30 tractor and two wooden Unadilla stave silos. He was an early innovator and was written about in Successful Farming Magazine. He claimed his secret of success was the two silos behind the barn and the superior diet he fed his cows. Not mentioned were the two hired men who did all the dirty work on the farm. Not that Mr. Schantz didn't work - he did all of the tractor driving and often worked late into the night in the barn.

So it went that fall, with Floyd accompanying Mr. Schantz on the night time hay deliveries. Gradually, Mr. Schantz left Floyd do more and more of the driving and he became quite good at shifting. He was one happy guy driving a big truck and earning some extra money. The schedule was always the same; Trenton track, off for a snack, the Freehold track, more grub, back to Trenton with the envelope, meet the men at Trenton again and bring another envelope home. Finally, as winter set in, Mr. Schantz left Floyd deliver the loads alone with instructions to follow the same pattern, ask no questions and be careful with the envelopes as they contained money.

One cold and windy night Floyd was thinking about his new girlfriend and decided to just skip the trip to Trenton and go directly to the Freehold race track, get his coffee and pie while the stable hands unloaded the hay, get the envelope in the usual manner and head home. He saved at least an hour and had time to ride past his lady friend's house to see if she had any other suitors. He parked the truck in Mr. Schantz's wagon shed and slid the envelope under the seat cushions as usual and went home to bed.

Next day, Mr. Schantz had four visitors in a big, blue Buick Phaeton. They had a long discussion with Mr. Schantz and then left. That night a funny thing happened. One of Mr. Schantz's silos blew all to smithereens. Tongue and groove cyprus boards were scattered all around like a tornado had hit and on the foundation where the silo stood was a mass of jumbled up copper tubing. Mr. Schantz told the neighbors that it was spontaneous combustion in the silo and he told Floyd that now he really didn't need him to drive truck anymore.

April Fool

Everybody in the whole township knew Harlan, and Harlan knew everybody in the township. As a matter of fact it was said that Harlan knew you before you were born. He knew everybody by their first name, to whom they were married and all of their relations for generations. Nosey-busyness was his business - for he was an extraordinary insurance man. This was before there was an insurance salesman on every block and long, long before insurance people merged, formed agencies, bought computers, hired office girls, played golf and forgot who you were – if they ever knew or cared.

Harlan had a little office building, an oak roll-top desk, a Burroughs adding machine, an Underwood typewriter and a great big safe. He also had a fantastic memory. On the other end of the town his brother had a Chevrolet and Allis Chalmers Farm Equipment Agency. He and his wife lived simply but well in their American- four-square home. Every two years he got a new car, including 1944 (the depths of World War Two,) when he got a brand new 1942 Chevy Fleetline 4-door sedan which his brother had squirreled away somewhere.

Harlan was a down to earth kind of guy and a most highly respected member of the community. He attended church regularly, donated lots of money to the fire company and gave a field behind his office to the town for a ball field for the kids. He could afford to do these things because everybody in the whole area bought their insurance from him. It was the thing to do - everybody did it! You knew Harlan; he knew you. You need insurance; Harlan sold it. That's the way things were.

He settled all claims promptly, in cash, with no questions asked. If you had a fender bender he would loan you a car and send the damaged vehicle to his brother's car agency. The body shop man there was an absolute genius with fender dollies and a spray gun. If you wanted a new car or a new piece of farm equipment and planned to buy it from his brother, Harlan would provide financing and you could pay him back every month. If you wanted to buy a farm, Harlan could handle that also, and if you couldn't make the monthly payments and he had to eventually foreclose, nobody knew the difference. People were allowed to stay on their farm as Harlan's sharecroppers.

He was a fair and well-liked person: a pillar of the community. And then it happened. The authorities took him away for a three year stay at Lewisburg Penitentiary.

Since he knew *everybody* in the community, Harlan insured *only* those whom he knew to be *poor* drivers, or to drink heavily, with the large nationwide insurance company which he represented. The other good folk paid modest premiums which he stuck in his safe. If anyone had a claim, Harlan paid promptly with no questions or insurance adjusters. Everybody was happy with the system until some bright insurance actuary realized that there were an uncommon number of claims from this one peaceful rural community and so sent out a couple of investigators.

They figured out that Harlan was doing precisely what insurance companies themselves do - excluding the high risk drivers and therefore making lots of money. The insurance company simply could not have that and reported him to the Internal Revenue people.

Harlan contended that the two million in his safe was "capital retains," set aside to pay off claims, (just like the big companies do) but the I.R.S. didn't believe him at all.

Hey, Hay!

Before our post-modern society, kids lived a much different life. No TVs, CDs, VCRs, DVDs, play stations, cell phones, iPods, or blogs. Also, no moms to haul them around in SUVs. After chores such as dumping the ashes, carrying coal or wood and feeding the chickens, kids were free. "You be back by suppertime," said mom and they were gone, off on their own to do their own thing. Baseball, football, cops and robbers, cowboys and Indians, fishing, swimming, exploring - and all just plain fun. Like Hereford calves they traveled in little herds, separate from the adult world. Innocent in many ways compared to today's kids, they knew far more about the real world because they could watch and sometimes participate in adult activities, i.e., real work.

Of great interest was the blacksmith shop (lots of new grammar), the sawmill with plenty of activity and the butcher shop (especially on killing day). Death and dying in the real world. Kids loved to hang around farms too. "Hey kid, go fetch that hammer hanging on the wall of the old cook house." "Kid, could you hold that cold chisel while I hit it with a sledge?" A meaningful experience. As long as kids were useful and not a nuisance they could stay and play with the cats, watch the baby goats and maybe feed the calves. So it was that one of the Howell kids was "helping" the Hartung family put up hay into the mow. He was sweeping up the hay seeds.

The Hartung family farm was, and still is, located in Roxburg, NJ. Ten thousand years ago the southernmost edge of the last glacier period was located in central Warren County, NJ. When glacial warming finally melted, it left its load of stone, hence the name, Roxburg. The Hartungs were good farmers and early innovators. They had an electric powered winch to power the hay rope. Neighbors used a plug horse or the old Chevy truck to hoist the loaded hayfork of loose hay up into the hay mow where the hired men spread it around and stomped it down.

Stewart Hartung used the nearly new Farmall F-14 to pull the loaded hay wagon up the ramp of the Pennsylvania–style bank barn onto what was the old threshing floor. Stewart then climbed up on the wagon, stabbed the U-shaped hayfork down into the load of hay and decided the wagon was not positioned properly. So he said to his sister, "Hey Gertrude, move the tractor ahead just a little bit." Like a flash, the Howell kid dropped his broom, jumped on to the idling F-14 and drove it right out the small barn door, (see photo). Stewart bailed out, Gertrude ran, and the Howell kid, who wasn't hurt, was not seen at the farm for several weeks.

Gottlieb

Gottlieb really liked cars, but he only owned three new cars in his lifetime. Only the rich upper class had owned automobiles when he had grown up in Switzerland. He came to America as a young man and walked or rode a bicycle to jobs on various farms. Eventually he rented a truck patch and got a Model TT Ford truck to deliver his vegetables to town. He saved every single cent and purchased a farm on Pinnacle Mountain. The farm had been abandoned and he worked all alone to grub out the briars and brambles so he could plant his crops. He also acquired some Brown Swiss calves and fixed the buildings.

Somehow, (and his son never did find out how), he met and married a Swiss girl who worked as a "nanny" in far off Nutley, NJ. They both worked hard and by 1937 bought a brand new Chevy Master Deluxe which lasted until he bought a new 1950 Buick Super. They went shopping Friday nights, perhaps to the movies Saturday nights, to church on Sunday and put very few miles on their cars. But when they went somewhere, they always dressed up, (in contrast to today's dressing down), just as the rich people had done back in the old country. But they never put on airs, they were the salt of the earth, the kind of people that made America great.

One day, on his way back from the hardware store in town, he noticed that his neighbor was pouring a cement driveway, so he stopped to help. (If you've ever worked cement on a hot summer day you know that you can always use extra help.) Gottlieb grabbed a trowel, knelt down and started to level out cement. When they got done and everybody stood up, they realized Gottlieb had been troweling his necktie in the cement; it quickly hardened, stiff as a board.

By 1964 they needed a new car and moved up the General Motors economic ladder to a new Cadillac. He kept it Simonized and covered up with old with old flannel sheets sewn together. They took a few vacation trips in the Cadillac and enjoyed semi–retirement for a few years. Then his wife died and his life came apart. He became a depressed and shriveled up old man. Years of hard work and spinal degeneration had made it so he could barely see over the Cadillac steering wheel. He went to town to pick out a tombstone for his wife and sideswiped some granite markers on display, ripping the whole right side of his car. He purchased a memorial stone, went home, ripped up his license and never drove again.

After a year he decided he would like to see the "old country" again before he died. His son took him to get a passport and to the airport, and Gottlieb flew for the first time - all alone. In Geneva he got a train to his home canton (county) and to the town where he was born. He rented a room, found a couple people who knew his cousins and met some old classmates. His cousins made a big fuss and had a family reunion. They took him around and visited his old haunts and he soon picked up the language he'd almost forgotten. Eventually he met a widow with whom he had gone to school – and they married. They bought Europasses and took an extended honeymoon, exploring Europe by rail. They lived happily ever after, and he never had to drive a car again, what with the excellent Swiss rail system.   But his last wish was that his ashes be sprinkled on his fields on Pinnacle Mountain, back in America.

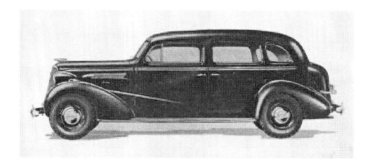

They Don't Make Em' Like They Used To

The 2012 cars are in the showrooms now and are touted as being infinitely superior to the 2011 models. Back in '02, they said the same thing about the 2001 cars and so ad infinitum. But are they any better?

Back in 1949 most car manufacturers had updated their styling and came out with new "improved" models. Of course there were guys who banged on the fenders and said, "They sure don't make them like they used to." And it was true, for cars of the 50's rode better, used no more fuel and lasted longer mechanically than their predecessors. They also used a lot more ornamental iron than cars of the 1920's did and then, of course, by the 1980's downsizing chopped off about 1½ feet from each end and about 700 lbs. of dead weight from all American cars.

In the 1920's 40,000 miles on an engine was a lot. By the 1940's cars went 75,000 miles before needing an overhaul. Today, 150,000 miles are common, but these are highway miles. Model T Fords were good for 15,000 miles and had no air cleaners or oil filters and there was a lot of dust and dirt back then to be sucked into the engine.

It's difficult to make a comparison. Model T Fords could not possibly attain modern highway speeds, let alone run for 150,000 miles. But modern cars sans filters wouldn't last on muddy, dusty, rutted roads carrying milk cans and chicken crates like Model T Fords did.

Of course, modern detergent lubricants have helped a lot. Any of us who tore down an engine prior to World War II had lots of black lard-like sludge to contend with. Also radial tires certainly ride better, last longer and don't squeal on turns.

Modern cars equipped with seat belts, air bags and antilock brakes are definitely safer, but there isn't much crumple zone surrounding the passenger compartment in today's cars.

In recent years auto manufacturers have coordinated design and manufacturing to make cars easier and cheaper to build. The result is that cars are much more difficult, if not impossible, for an owner to service. It is said that if the head of General Motors engineering had a new car quit running he would have to call Mr. Goodwrench just like anybody else would. Personally, I like it when you open the hood and you can look down and see the ground.

Cars use less gas today as a result of the oil embargo scare in the 1970's. They also produce less pollution thanks to catalytic converters. But the fumes from oxygenated fuel are pretty bad stuff indeed!

Therefore after considering all of the above I conclude that modern cars are indeed better than ever for today's driving conditions. But it sure is nice to get up into my Model T for just plain happy fun motoring. It is equally nice to get into my 1950 Olds 98, look out over that long hood with a big V8 underneath, sit on nice soft cushioned seats and have room for five (or seven) other people to stretch their legs.

Like the man said, "They don't make 'em like they used to!"

Peasant Pride

I'm not proud and never have been.

Well, maybe I'd better hedge that a bit. When at the age of 68, I first became a grandfather, I was pretty proud. But, in general, I don't think I've been pompous and proud. If it runs and gets the job done, that's just fine with me.

I don't bleed green and rave about my John Deere stuff and my red blood has nothing to do with CNH International red paint. I've owned perhaps a dozen canines and I am a bit partial to my Australian red heeler. Over the years I acquired Ford, Chevy, GMC and Dodge trucks; some good and some not so good.

Probably my worst vehicle was a Dodge four wheel drive pick-up truck built in the mid 1970's. It was not a power wagon. With its oxidized orange paint we called it the "pumpkin wagon." Perhaps you recall the bird bath hoods. The stylists made the top of the hood concaved and so after every rain the water puddled in the center of the hood until it evaporated or somebody moved the thing.

Farm dogs Barney and John in the "Pumpkin Wagon" Dodge

That Dodge did manage to get the job done, but just barely. The only thing good about the vehicle was its dash. The same brilliant industrial designer who dreamed up the hood made the entire area above the gauges into a shelf the full width of the cab. It measured at least eighteen inches from the edge to the windshield and it held my life's possessions close at hand, which included, but not limited to: a penknife, a calculator, several gloves, a seed corn hat, ballpoint pens, cow marking crayons, sun glasses, a can opener, vise grips, a thermometer, calf obstetrical chains, ear tags, welding rods, exacto-knives, an electric-fence tester, dog biscuits, cough drops, a flashlight, several screw drivers and a roll of duct tape. The best part was that the whole shelf sloped 45 degrees toward the windshield, so that none of my possessions ever bounced off, even when chasing calves uphill out of the meadow with all four wheels spinning. My stuff just laid there. I wasn't proud about having all my valuable possessions on display; I just liked having them handy.

I do have a restored 1917 Model T Ford Touring and I must admit I'm a bit proud of it. I had to do some repair work on the T and finally got it running one warm February day and decided to take the grandkids for their very first antique car ride. I left the Model T running, "puggidy, puggidy, puggidy" and went into the house. I got my daughter-in-law's permission, found sneakers and parkas, stuffed the kids into them, went back outside and loaded the kids into the back seat. I got in myself, pushed in on the left (low gear) pedal... and stalled it!

I got out and cranked. My daughter-in-law took pictures. I cranked some more. Nothing. Not even a pop! Getting short of breath, I had to admit defeat. "Everybody out of the car" I said, a bit disappointed. Five year old Caleb, who was just learning to read, looked down at the Ford script embossed in the Model T running board and said, "Humph... It's a Ford."

You know, I must confess, it kind of hurt my pride.

Abe (with arm raised) and Caleb watch humbled Grandpa crank the Model T.

Where I'm From

Born in the front bedroom of the my great-grandparent's farmhouse.
Playing in a cardboard box during milking time.
Damming up a trickle from a summer shower with my cast iron bulldozer and toy Mack truck.
Crawling under the rhubarb leaves trying to catch kittens.
Hiding under the porch with the dog to see which one of us my folks missed first.
Feeding the chickens.
Watching the bull run after the heifers.
Pulling corn husks.
Tugging on the flywheel of the John Deere A.
Shoveling corn out of a crib and smelling rats (they smell like popcorn).*
Milking Holsteins.

Meeting, courting, marrying somebody special.
Two kids, two grandkids, all living here with me on the home place for so long that somehow when I travel, the sun, stars and moon don't seem to be in quite the right place.

*Editor's note: Bob Frey doesn't like popcorn.